Big Farms, Little Farms

A Visual Guide to Farm Animals and Machinery

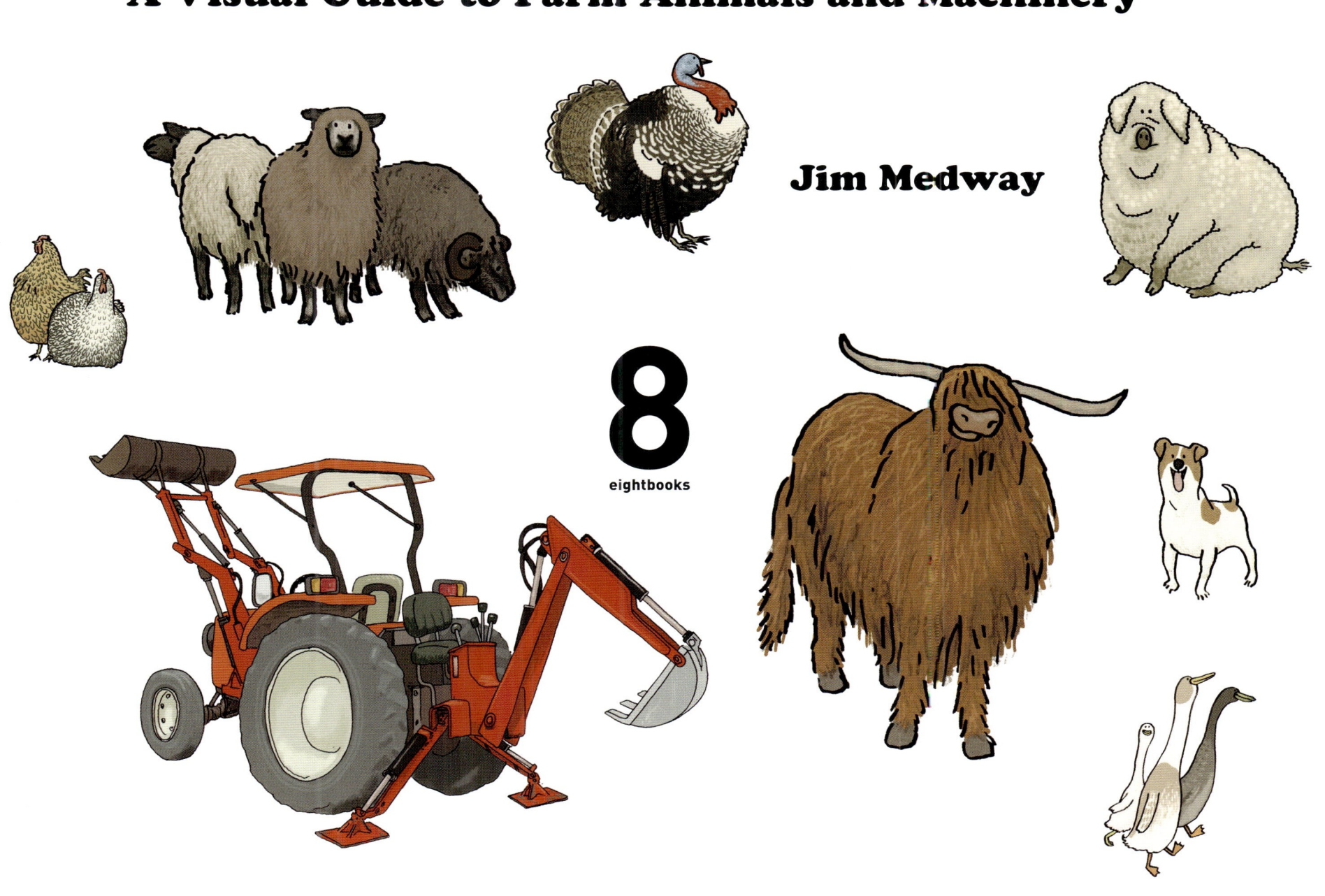

Jim Medway

8
eightbooks

Contents

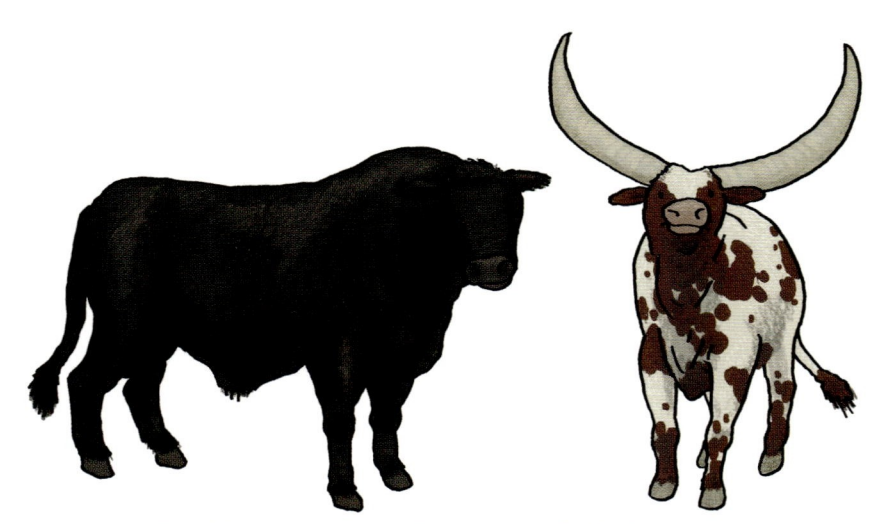

Cattle and Cow Milking
Cattle are farmed for their meat, milk and hides. Some cattle breeds, like the Hereford, are bred for their beef, while others, like the Jersey, are dairy cattle bred for their milk. 4–7

Sheep and Sheep Farming
Most farmers breed sheep for lamb meat, but wool is still a valuable product. In ancient times sheep were kept for their milk and skins. 8–11

Pigs and Pig Farming
Domestic pigs are bred for their meat, such as bacon, pork and ham. Pigs are omnivores (they will eat every kind of food), and in the wild they will forage. 12–15

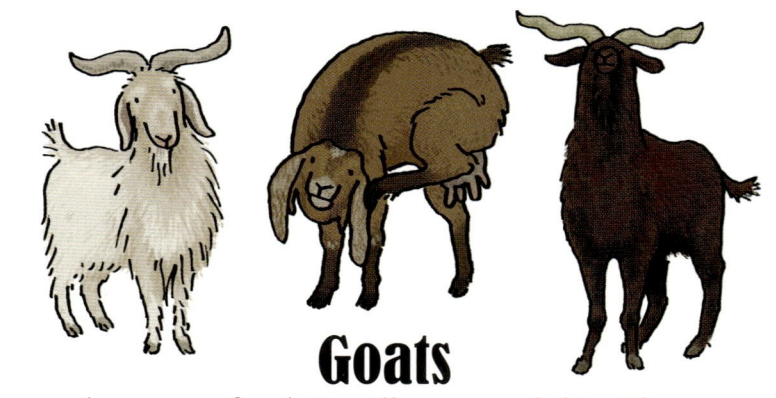

Goats
Farmers keep goats for their milk, meat and skin. They are used mainly in Asia and Africa, particularly in India, China and Nigeria. 16–17

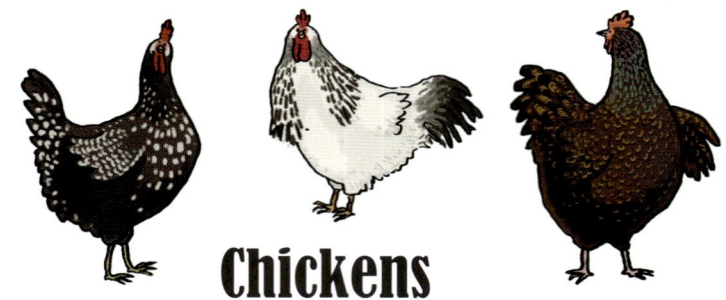

Chickens
Chickens are bred for their eggs and meat. Chicken eggs can be white, brown or blue. There are hundreds of different breeds in lots of different colours. 18–19

Ducks and Geese
Ducks and geese were once very important animals on farms. Their feathers were plucked many times a year and used to stuff furniture and bedding. They are still bred for meat. 20

Turkeys
Turkeys were first domesticated by Spanish settlers in North America more than 500 years ago. Today most turkeys are farmed for their meat in huge factories. 21

Dogs
Farmers have always kept dogs. Today they use sheepdogs mainly for herding, but once they used dogs to protect their animals from predators such as wolves. 22–23

Tractors
The tractor was first used over 100 years ago. Today the tractor is still the most common vehicle on farms and is used for pulling and pushing agricultural machinery. 24–25

Farm Machinery
Farmers use huge wheeled machines to help them dig, pick and cut fruit and vegetables, such as carrots, olives, grapes, potatoes, corn and sugarcane. 26–27

Index
Fun-packed index full of fascinating facts about animals and farm machines. 28–31

Cattle

Simmental

Holstein Friesian

Charolais

Texas Longhorn

Aberdeen Angus

Galloway

Jersey

Gelbvieh

Hereford Bull

Ankole-Watusi

Dexter

Brahman

Brown Swiss

Shorthorn

Scottish Highland

Limousin

Cow Milking

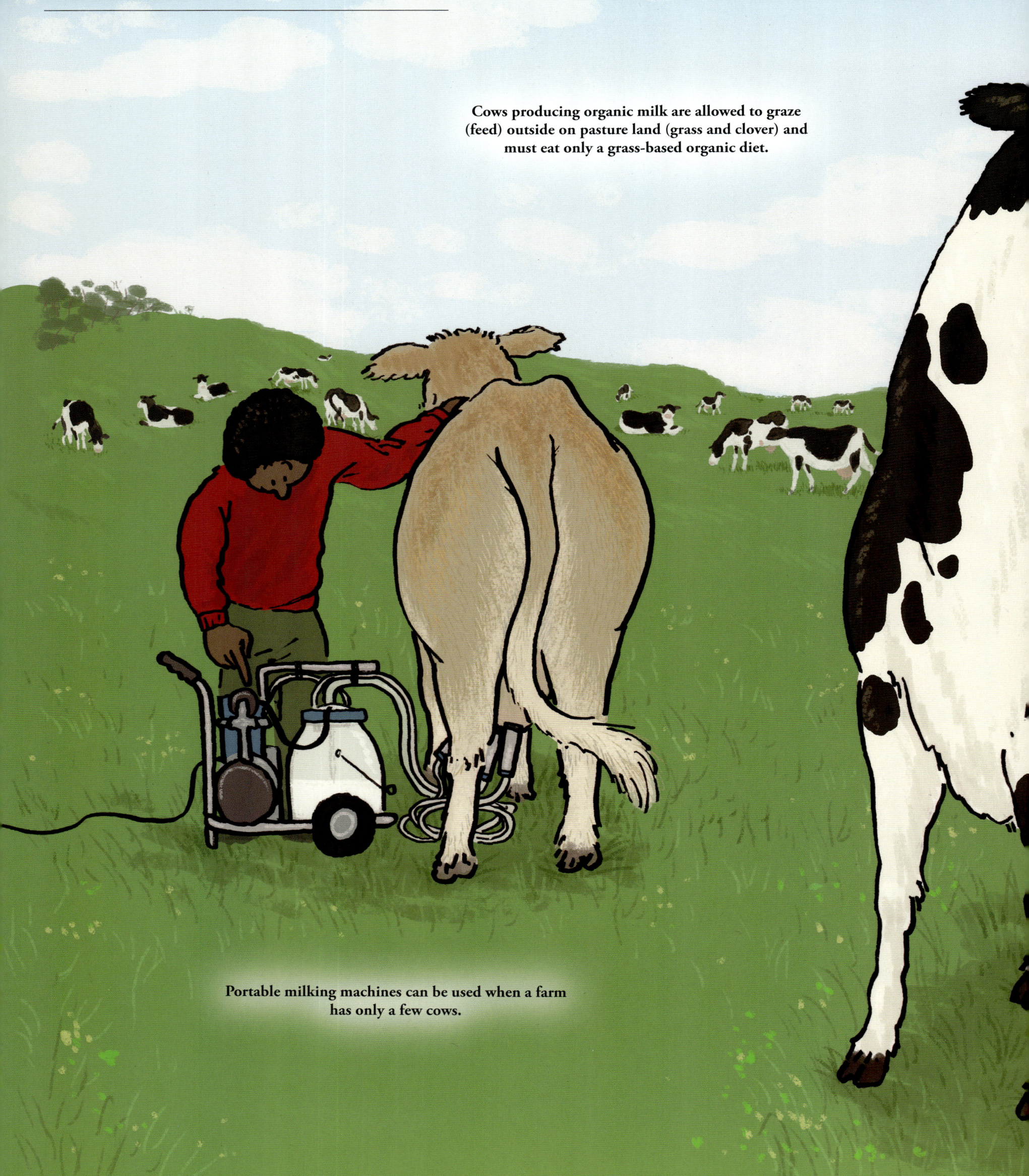

Cows producing organic milk are allowed to graze (feed) outside on pasture land (grass and clover) and must eat only a grass-based organic diet.

Portable milking machines can be used when a farm has only a few cows.

Originally all cows were milked by hand. Today few farmers still milk by hand.

Today most cows are milked using automatic milking machines. Milk is used to make butter, cream, cheese and yogurt.

Sheep

Lincoln

Rambouillet

Montadale

Texel

Targhee

Romney

American Blackbelly

Merino

Katahdin

Border Leicester

Suffolk

Dorset

Hampshire

Cheviot

Scottish Blackface

Dorper

Jacob

Southdown

East Friesian

Shetland

Sheep Farming

Sheep dipping – farmers dip their sheep in a special liquid to protect them from parasites such as ticks and lice.

Lamb feeding – sometimes lambs need to be fed by a bottle if their mothers can't give them milk.

Farmers use specially trained sheepdogs to round up their herds for shearing and dipping or moving to new fields. Organic sheep should graze in rotation with cattle.

Sheep shearing – normally sheep have their coats "shorn" once a year. Their wool can be made into clothing or carpets. 500 years ago wool was the most important product from sheep. Today sheep are bred mainly for their meat.

Pigs

British Saddleback

Tamworth

Gascon

Gloucester Old Spots

Red Wattle

Duroc

Berkshire

Vietnamese Pot-bellied

Swabian-Hall

Kunekune

Guinea Hog

Basque

Nero dei Nebrodi

American Yorkshire

Iberian

Large Black

Mangalitsa

Meishan

Benthiem Black Pied

Husum Red Pied

Oxford Sandy and Black

Hampshire

13

Pig Farming

Farmers keep pigs in pens or in open fields where they have shelters to protect them from bad weather.

200 years ago pigs lived and grazed in woods. Today organic pigs are kept in family groups and allowed to have access to fields. When indoors they should be given straw bedding.

Typically a sow (female pig) will have as many as 10 piglets.

Goats

Boer

Saanen

Alpine

Nigerian Dwarf

Pygmy

Kiko

Spanish

Lamancha

Toggenburg

Kalahari Red

Verata

Angora

Kinder

Tennessee Fainting

Golden Guernsey

Anglo-Nubian

Oberhasli

Black Bengal

Rangeland

Chickens

Orpington

Cochin

Ancona

Plymouth Rock

Ameraucana

Rhode Island Red

Buff Orpington

Hamburg

Leghorn

Barnevelder

New Hampshire

Australorp

Wyandotte

Marans

Red Star

Sussex

Brahma

Silkie

Ducks and Geese

- African goose
- White Pekin duck
- Call duck
- Indian Runner duck
- Aylesbury duck
- Buff Orpington goose
- Hook Bill duck
- Pomeranian goose
- Toulouse goose
- Roman tufted goose
- Ancona duck
- Sebastopol goose
- Buff Orpington duck
- Muscovy duck
- Chinese goose

Turkeys

Narragansett

White Holland

Blue Slate

Bourbon Red

Standard Bronze

Black

Broad Breasted White

Dogs

German Shepherd

Border Collie

Berger Picard

Giant Schnauzer

Australian Cattle Dog

Bernese Mountain

Maremma Sheepdog

Old English Sheepdog

Australian Shepherd

Tibetan Mastiff

English Shepherd

Pembroke Welsh Corgi

Jack Russell Terrier

Great Pyrenees

Komondor

Anatolian Shepherd

Tractors

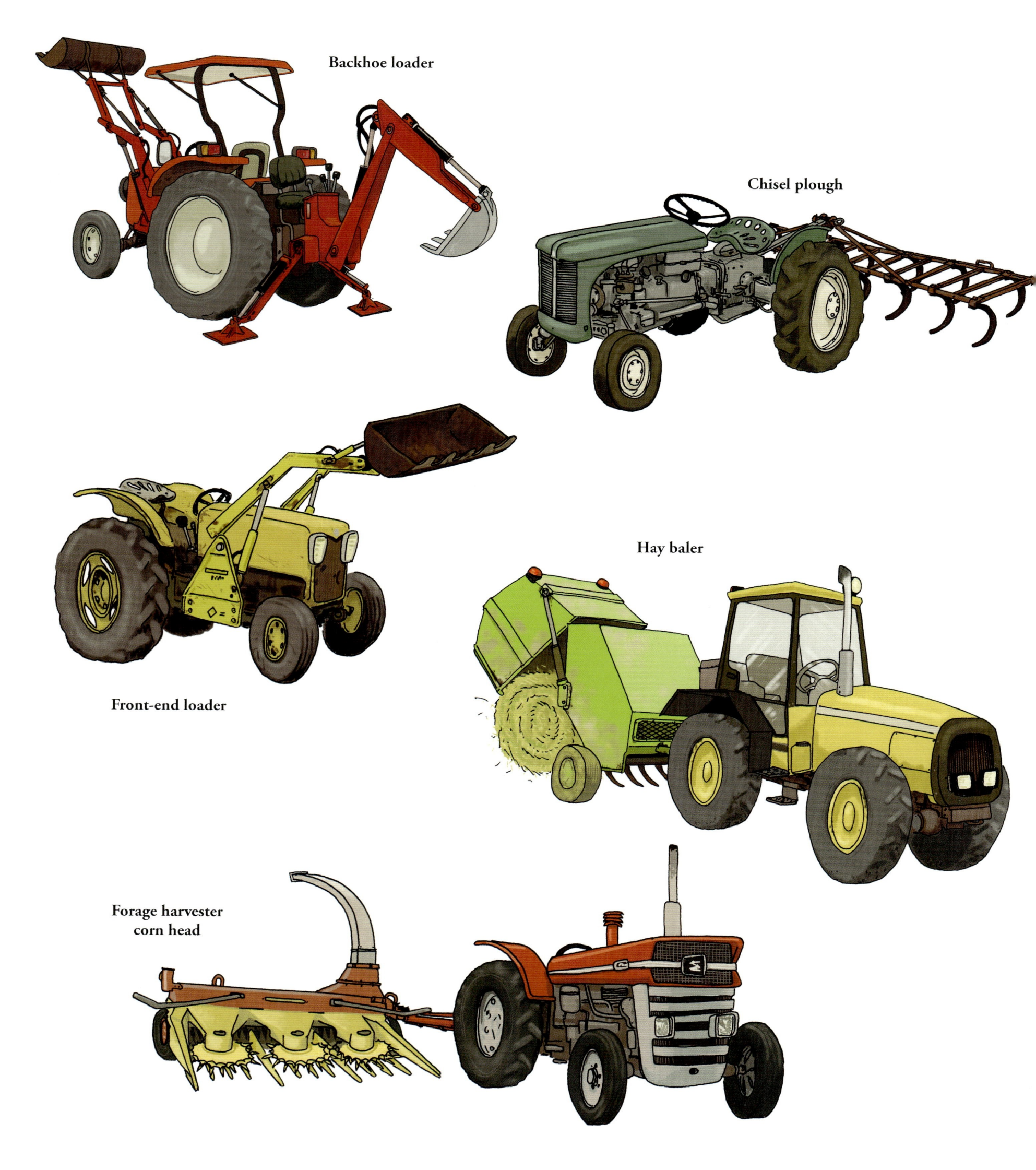

Backhoe loader

Chisel plough

Front-end loader

Hay baler

Forage harvester corn head

Slurry tanker

Hedge cutter

Harrow

Seed drill

Grain cart

Farm Machinery

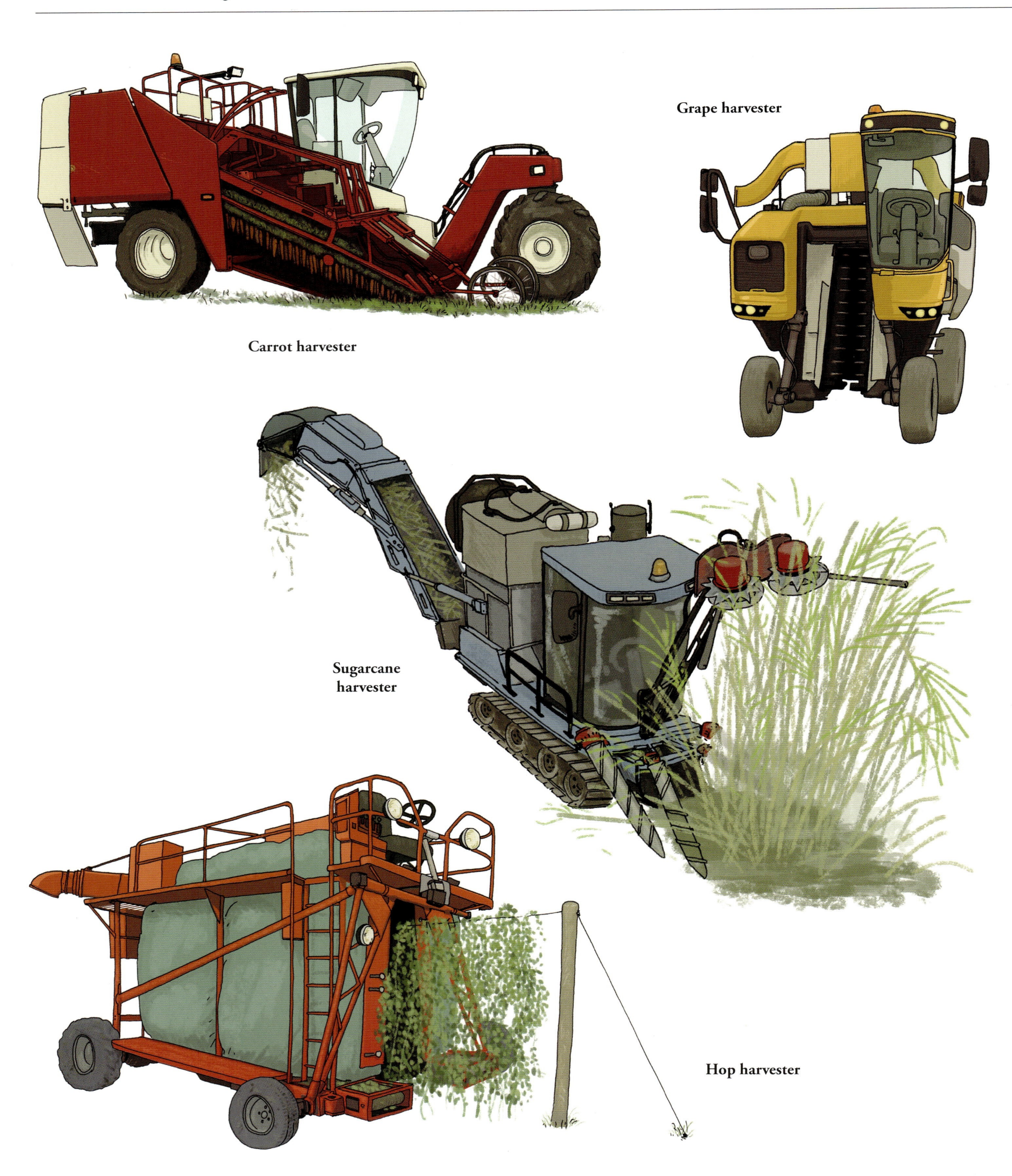

Grape harvester

Carrot harvester

Sugarcane harvester

Hop harvester

Corn harvester

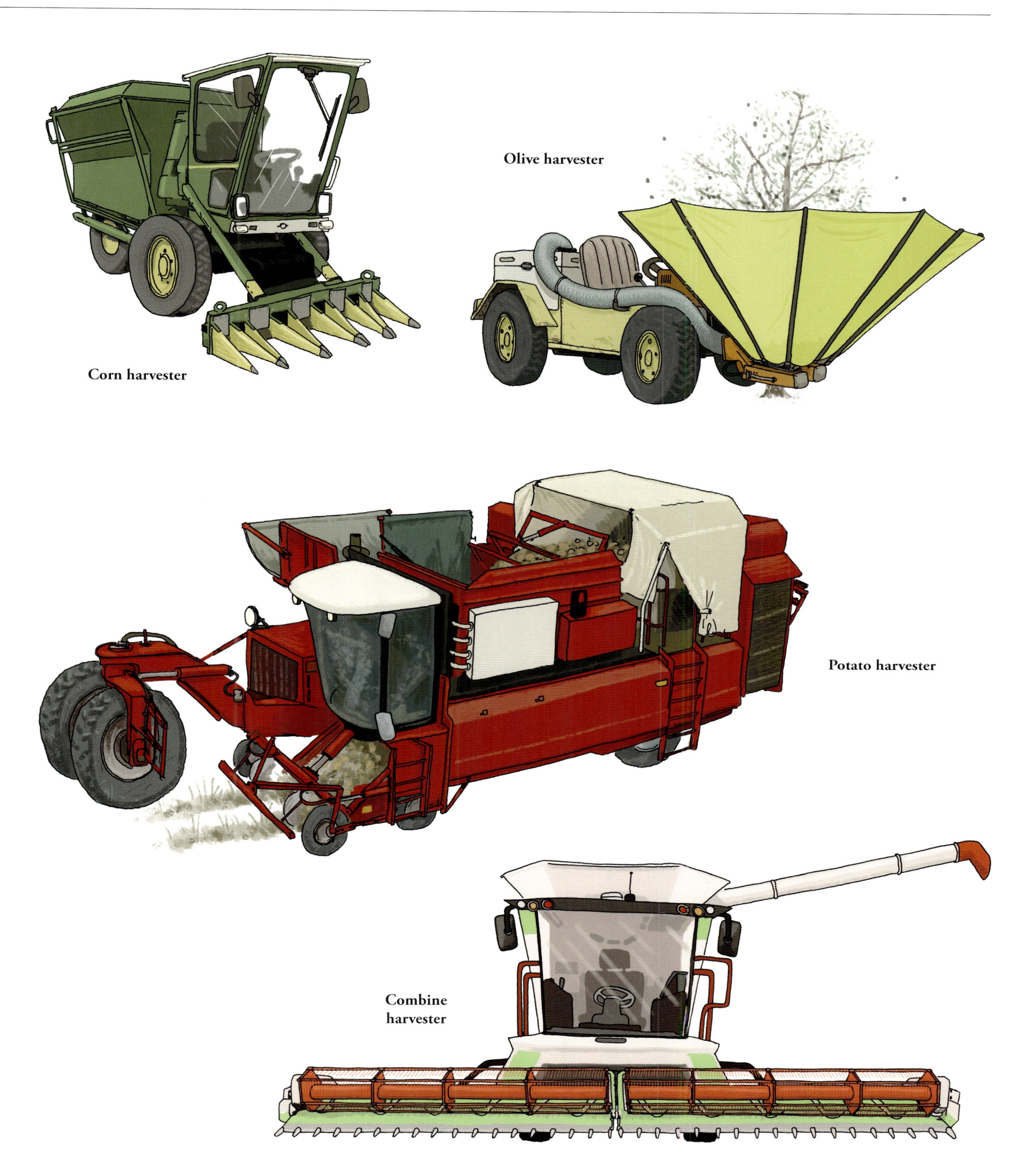

Olive harvester

Potato harvester

Combine harvester

27

Index

Aberdeen Angus cattle
These cattle come from Scotland and are able to survive in very harsh places where it is cold, snowy and windy. 4

African goose
The African goose is descended from the Swan goose. In spite of its name it most probably came from China. 20

Alpine goat
Alpine goats originated in the French Alps. Their milk can be used to make butter, cheese and ice cream. 16

Ameraucana chicken
The Ameraucana is one of the few breeds of chicken to lay blue eggs. 18

American Blackbelly sheep
The American Blackbelly sheep has a face with colours similar to the badger's. The rams (male sheep) have very impressive curled horns. 8

American Yorkshire pig
The most popular pig in the United States, the American Yorkshire has smaller and floppier ears than the English Yorkshire pig to which it is related. 13

Anatolian Shepherd dog
This large and powerful dog comes from Anatolia (central Turkey) and is used to protect livestock. In packs it can chase down and kill predators such as wolves. 23

Ancona chicken
Named after the Italian city of Ancona, from which it originates, today this chicken is now common in Britain and the United States. 18

Ancona duck
The Ancona duck is from England and is pied in colour, which means it has random colour patches that can be black, blue, or brown on white. 20

Anglo-Nubian goat
The Anglo-Nubian goat has long, floppy ears and a round-shaped nose. One of its nicknames is "Rabbit Goat" because of its ears. It is bred for its milk and meat. 17

Angora goat
Angora goats produce a very soft fleece (coat) called mohair that is used to make jumpers. These goats originated in Turkey. 17

Ankole-Watusi
This very old breed – used by the Ancient Egyptians – comes from Africa and has the largest horns of any cattle in the world. 5

Australian Cattle Dog
This tough and very active dog works on huge farms to help herd cattle. 22

Australian Shepherd dog
The name is misleading: this animal originated in the United States during the Gold Rush in the 1840s. It is closely related to the Border Collie. 23

Australorp chicken
This black chicken originates from Australia and its name comes from "Australian Black Orpington". 19

Aylesbury duck
A white domesticated duck, the Aylesbury comes originally from Buckinghamshire in England. In the 18th century Aylesburys were walked to market in London more than 40 miles (64km) away. 20

Backhoe loader
This type of tractor is used for digging. It has a loader, or large shovel, on the front and a backhoe, or digger, at the back. 24

Barnevelder chicken
This is a Dutch breed of domestic chicken that was created by crossing Dutch chickens with chickens from Asia. 19

Basque pig
From the Basque country, an area in northwest Spain and southwest France, this pig is piebald, which means it has black and white spots on its skin. 13

Bentheim Black Pied pig
This is a rare breed from an area in Germany named Bentheim. It has white and black spots and drooping ears. 13

Berger Picard dog
Believed to be the oldest of French sheepdog breeds, the Berger Picard has quite a scruffy appearance with a tousled coat. 22

Berkshire pig
Berkshire pigs have black bodies and white "points" on their feet and snouts. Napoleon in George Orwell's novel *Animal Farm* is a Berkshire pig. 12

Bernese Mountain dog
This farm dog from the Alps in Switzerland has a particular colouring – a white and black coat with red markings. 22

Black Bengal goat
The Black Bengal goat comes from Bangladesh and northeast India. It is a popular animal among the poor because it doesn't need a lot of food. 17

Black turkey
Black turkeys were originally brought to Europe from Aztec Mexico by Spanish explorers. They are thought to be the oldest breed of turkey in Britain. 21

Blue Slate turkey
Blue Slate turkeys are a beautiful ash-grey colour. They were first bred in the United States in the 19th century. 21

Boer goat
Originally from South Africa, where they were bred by tribespeople, Boer goats are stockily built and have short legs. 16

Border Collie dog
The Collie is a very old breed of sheepdog. It is believed to have first been used by the Celts in the time of the Ancient Romans. 22

Border Leicester sheep
The Border Leicester is a British breed of sheep from Northumberland. It has long wool and no horns. 8

Bourbon Red turkey
The Bourbon Red turkey comes from Bourbon County, Kentucky in the United States. It has dark red feathers on its body and white feathers on its wings. 21

Brahma chicken
Famous for its large size, the Brahma chicken is known as "The King of Chickens". 19

Brahman cattle
This American cattle breed is known to be very docile and intelligent. It is also very large. 5

British Saddleback pig
This breed of pig was created by mixing two breeds, the Essex Saddleback and the Wessex Saddleback. It's called a Saddleback because it has a white strip or "saddle" around its body and front legs. 12

Broad Breasted White turkey
These are the most widely used turkeys in the world. They are unable to fly and sadly are prone to diseases. 21

Brown Swiss cattle
Considered one of the oldest dairy cattle breeds, these beautiful brown cows come from the northeast of Switzerland. 5

Buff Orpington chicken
The Buff Orpington is an English breed of chicken with light brown (buff) feathers. 19

Buff Orpington duck
The Buff Orpington is used for eggs and meat. As its name suggests it is a buff – light brown – colour. The bill of the drake (male) is yellow, while the beak of the hen (female) is brown. 20

Call duck
Call ducks used to be kept by farmers who would use the birds' calls and quacks to attract other ducks towards hunters' guns. Today they are kept mainly as pets because of their small size. 20

Carrot harvester
The carrot harvester makes picking carrots easy by pulling them from the ground by their stems. It then cleans off any mud and cuts off the leaves. 26

Charolais cattle
One of the most famous beef cattle breeds, Charolais came originally from France. They are usually a creamy-white colour. 4

Cheviot sheep
The Cheviot sheep comes from the hills of Northumberland in northern England and the Scottish borders. It was first bred for its wool, which was used in the tweed mills of Scotland. 9

Chinese goose
This white or brown goose comes from China and is well known for laying lots of eggs – as many as 50–60 over a breeding season. 20

Chisel plough
A chisel plough is used to dig up fields so that the soil can be loosened and seeds can be planted in the earth. 24

Cochin chicken
The Cochin chicken is unusual because its feathers cover both its body and its legs. It originates from China. 18

Combine harvester
This huge machine is used to gather wheat crops. Wheat is the most widely eaten grain in the world. 27

Corn harvester
A corn harvester is used to harvest corn and prepare it for storage. 27

Dexter cattle
Dexters are the smallest of European cattle breeds. They originated in Ireland and are descended from the black cattle of the Celts. 5

Dorper sheep
From South Africa, the Dorper has a very short coat of wool, a black face and a white body. 9

Dorset sheep
Alternatively known as the Dorset Horn, this sheep can breed throughout the winter. 9

Duroc pig
This breed is the least aggressive type of pig raised for meat. Durocs come from New England in the United States and are red with drooping ears. 12

East Friesian sheep
From northern Germany, East Friesian sheep are bred mainly to produce milk. They have pink noses. 9

English Shepherd dog
This sheepdog was developed in the United States from farm dogs brought by settlers from England and Scotland in the 17th and 18th centuries. 23

Forage harvester with corn head
Forage harvesters are machines which gather plants that can be fed to cattle. This particular variety is specially modified to cut and collect cereal grain. 24

Front-end loader
A front-end loader is used for heavy digging and for lifting logs, snow, earth, gravel, animal feed or other material. 24

Galloway cattle
The Galloway breed of cattle came originally from Scotland. That helps to explain its thick coat, which protects it from the cold climate in the mountains there. 4

Gascon pig
Originally from remote and mountainous regions of France, the Gascon is probably that country's most ancient pig breed. 12

Gelbvieh cattle
The name "Gelbvieh" means "yellow cattle" in German. This breed comes from Bavaria. 4

German Shepherd dog
One of the world's most popular dog breeds, the Alsatian (as it is also known) is highly intelligent and is used by the police and the army. 22

Giant Schnauzer dog
A German working dog, the Giant Schnauzer was first used to drive livestock to market and protect farms. Schnauzers have distinctive beards. 22

Gloucester Old Spots pig
Also known as "Orchard Pigs" because they were traditionally kept in orchards, this breed has black spots over a pink body. 12

Golden Guernsey goat
Golden Guernseys are named for their distinctive color and for the island in the English Channel from which they originated. They are very sweet and friendly. 17

Grain cart
A grain cart is also called a chaser bin. It is used to transport harvested grain from fields to grain trucks. 25

Grape harvester
Grape harvesters are big machines that use rubber sticks to get grapes to drop off vines onto a conveyor belt. 26

Great Pyrenees dog
Once known as the Royal Dog of France, the big, fluffy, white Great Pyrenees was bred to protect sheep from predators in the mountains. 23

Guinea Hog pig
The Guinea Hog is a small, black breed of pig that comes from the United States. 12

Hamburg chicken
This German breed of chicken was mentioned in Geoffrey Chaucer's *The Nun's Priest's Tale*. It lays white eggs. 18

Hampshire pig
This American breed was first imported from Hampshire in England. It is one of the most important pig breeds in the world because it is large, heavily muscled and grows quickly. 13

Hampshire sheep
Also called the Hampshire Downs, this sheep is calm and quiet. It has rivers of wool over its head which give it an interesting face. 9

Harrow
A harrow is used to break up soil and make the surface of the field smoother and have fewer lumps. 25

Hay baler
A hay baler cuts hay (grass) and then compresses it into rectangular or cylindrical bales that are held in shape with twine or wire. 24

Hedge cutter
On farms with lots of fields, hedges have to be cut to stop them getting too high. In England hedges can be cut only in late autumn and winter to protect nesting birds. 25

Hereford cattle
Hereford cattle are famous for their beef. Originally from the county of Herefordshire in England, today there are more than 5 million of them around the world. 5

Holstein Friesian cattle
The most common type of cattle in Europe, these black-and-white cows produce huge quantities of milk. 4

Hook Bill duck
This very old breed of duck used to live on the canals in the Netherlands. It has a distinctive curved beak. 20

Hop harvester
Hops are used to flavour beer. They are cut and collected by this special machine. 26

Husum Red Pied pig
At the start of the 20th century, Danes living under Prussian rule were not allowed to show their flag, so instead they bred this pig, which has a white horizontal band across a red body and resembles the Danish flag, hence its other name: the Danish Protest pig. 13

Iberian pig
A breed from Spain and Portugal, Iberian pigs are usually black in colour. Traditionally they are fed on acorns. 13

Index

Indian Runner duck
These domestic ducks came from Indonesia. They stand tall and upright and, unlike most ducks, they run rather than waddle. They cannot fly and don't make nests, instead laying eggs wherever they happen to be. 20

Jack Russell Terrier dog
Jack Russell Terriers were first bred to be used on foxhunts to flush out foxes. They quickly became popular farm dogs because of their ability as ratters. 23

Jacob sheep
This unusual-looking sheep is piebald (black and white) and often has four horns. It was first used as a park sheep to look pretty on country estates in England. 9

Jersey cattle
These are dairy cattle from Jersey, one of the Channel Islands near France. Their milk is famous for being very high in butterfat and being slightly yellow in colour. 4

Kalahari Red goat
A red goat from the Kalahari Desert in South Africa, this animal is used mainly for meat. 16

Katahdin sheep
The Katahdin sheep is a meat sheep from the United States. It does not need to be sheared, because every year it sheds its winter coat naturally. 8

Kiko goat
The Kiko goat comes from New Zealand. "Kiko" is the Māori word for meat. 16

Kinder goat
From Washington State in the United States, the Kinder goat was created by crossing a Pygmy goat with an Anglo-Nubian goat. 17

Komondor dog
The Komondor has an amazing, long, white, corded coat. It was used as a sheepdog in Hungary, where it is considered a national treasure. 23

Kunekune pig
This small, hairy pig comes from New Zealand. Kunekunes are very easy to maintain and were once kept by Māoris. 12

Lamancha goat
Lamancha goats come from California in the United States – they have very short ears. 16

Large Black pig
The Large Black is Britain's only black breed of pig. The dark colour of its skin means that it doesn't get sunburnt like pink pigs and so is well suited to very hot climates. 13

Leghorn chicken
White Leghorn chickens are bred for their eggs. They originated in Italy, which is why they are called Leghorn, the English name for the city of Livorno. 18

Limousin cattle
From the west of France, Limousin are highly muscled red cattle. They were originally bred to pull carts, but today are farmed for their meat. 5

Lincoln sheep
Also known as the Lincoln Longwool because of its long coat, this sheep produces the heaviest and longest fleece in the world. 8

Mangalitsa pig
The Mangalitsa is a very unusual pig because it grows a thick woolly coat similar to that of a sheep. 13

Marans chicken
From Marans, a port town in France, this chicken lays very dark brown eggs. 19

Maremma Sheepdog
A big, white dog, the Maremma comes from Italy, where it was once used to protect flocks of sheep from wolves and bears. 22

Meishan pig
From China, the Meishan pig is quite a rare breed. It has large, drooping ears and wrinkled black skin. 13

Merino sheep
Originating in Spain more than 800 years ago, the Merino sheep is famous for having some of the softest wool in the world. 8

Montadale sheep
This sheep comes from the Midwest of the United States. It has white wool with black nostrils and hooves. 8

Muscovy duck
Muscovy ducks are sometimes called "Barbary" ducks. They come from Central and South America. They were first domesticated by Native Americans. 20

Narragansett turkey
The Narragansett has spectacular plumage – grey, black, tan and white feathers. It is believed to be a cross between a wild turkey and a domesticated turkey. 21

Nero dei Nebrodi pig
The name means "black from Nebrodi" – this black pig comes from the Italian island of Sicily. 13

New Hampshire chicken
From New Hampshire in the United States, this is a red coloured chicken that is related to the Rhode Island Red. 19

Nigerian Dwarf goat
This intelligent and gentle goat comes from West Africa, but is bred in North America for its milk. 16

Oberhasli goat
This American goat has a brown coat and a black face – this colouring is called "chamoisee" because it looks like the Chamois goat from Switzerland. 17

Old English Sheepdog
This lovely big, shaggy dog loves to herd animals and is famous for its gentle, calm and affectionate nature. 22

Olive harvester
The olive harvester is a machine that shakes the tree and then catches all the olives in large yellow flaps before sucking them up. 27

Orpington chicken
From the town in Orpington in Kent, England, this large chicken has fluffed-out feathers. 18

Oxford Sandy and Black pig
One of the oldest British pig breeds, the Oxford Sandy and Black has pale skin with black spots. It is also called the "Plum Pudding Pig" because of its appearance. 13

Pembroke Welsh Corgi dog
Queen Elizabeth II of England's favourite breed, Pembroke Welsh corgis were originally bred as herding dogs for cattle. They would nip at the heels of cows to keep them moving. 23

Plymouth Rock chicken
These are one of America's oldest chicken breeds and they have black and white plumage (feathers). 18

Pomeranian goose
The grey or buff Pomeranian goose is very popular in Poland and Germany. 20

Potato harvester
Potato harvesters are machines that dig out potatoes. They sieve out the loose soil from the potatoes before moving them into a trailer via a side elevator. 27

Pygmy goat
The Pygmy is a miniature type of goat and is often kept as a pet. It likes to jump and is known to be affectionate. 16

Rambouillet sheep
Also known as the French Merino, this sheep was first raised on the royal farm at Rambouillet southwest of Paris in the 18th century. 8

Rangeland goat
These goats were introduced to Australia by Europeans. They are tall and broad and have short hair. 17

Red Star chicken
The Red Star chicken was bred to lay a lot of eggs. It is an American chicken. 19

Red Wattle pig
From the United States, these red-coloured pigs have wattles, or tassels, that hang down from their necks. No one knows why they have these flaps of skin. 12

Rhode Island Red chicken
This chicken comes from Rhode Island in the United States and is famous for its ability to lay a lot of brown eggs – 200–300 a year. 18

Roman Tufted goose
One of the oldest goose breeds in the world, this bird has a little tuft or crest on its head. 20

Romney sheep
Romney sheep came originally from Kent in England, but today are found mainly in New Zealand. They have wool that grows over their legs. 8

Saanen goat
A Swiss breed of domesticated goat, the Saanen has white skin and short white hair. 16

Scottish Blackface sheep
The Scottish Blackface is the most common sheep in Britain, where there are over 1 million ewes (females) of the breed. 9

Scottish Highland cattle
Scottish Highland cattle have very long horns and long, woolly red coats. This ancient breed is believed to be over 1,500 years old. 5

Sebastopol goose
A lovely-looking goose, the Sebastopol has curly white feathers over its back and smooth feathers over its neck. 20

Seed drill
A seed drill is pulled by a tractor and used to sow the seed for crops. Hollow blades dig holes in the soil, and seeds are then dropped into the holes before being covered in soil. 25

Shetland sheep
Originally from the Shetland Isles in Scotland, these sheep can survive in mountainous conditions where there is little to eat. 9

Shorthorn cattle
Shorthorn cattle come from northeast England. They can be red, white or roan (a mixture of red and white). 5

Silkie chicken
An unusual-looking chicken, the Silkie has very fluffy plummage that feels like silk and covers its head and body. 19

Simmental cattle
Originally from Switzerland, the Simmental breed of cattle is known to be very docile in nature. 4

Slurry tanker
Slurry is made of waste materials from crops and animals. It is used to fertilise fields to make crops grow faster. 25

Southdown sheep
This old breed comes from the English county of Sussex, where in the 14th century there were perhaps as many as 100,000 of them. 9

Spanish goat
Spanish goats were brought into the United States from Spain via Mexico. They are very useful because they will eat unwanted plants on pastures. 16

Standard Bronze turkey
The Standard Bronze turkey was first bred in the 18th century and was one of the most popular turkeys to eat in the United States until the middle of the 20th century, when it was overtaken by the Broad Breasted White. 21

Suffolk sheep
From the east of England, the Suffolk is a large sheep with black face and legs. 9

Sussex chicken
From the county of Sussex in England, this is one of the oldest breeds of chicken in Britain. 19

Sugarcane harvester
Sugarcane, which is used to make sugar, is cut using this special machine that clasps the stalks at the base before stripping off the leaves and then cutting the sugarcane into segments. 26

Swabian-Hall pig
This rare German breed of pig has a black head and bottom with a pink strip over its body. It was first bred in the 18th century by King George III of England. 12

Tamworth pig
This is thought to be Britain's oldest pure breed of pig. It comes from the town of Tamworth in the county of Staffordshire. 12

Targhee sheep
Targhee sheep are very hardy and have adapted to living in the mountain ranges of the western United States. 8

Tennessee Fainting goat
When this goat is startled it will become very stiff and fall over on the spot as if it were fainting. 17

Texas Longhorn cattle
These cattle are the descendants of the animals brought to the Americas by Christopher Columbus and the Spanish. They have huge horns and can be many different colours. 4

Texel sheep
These short-tailed sheep originated in Texel, an island off the coast of the Netherlands. 8

Tibetan Mastiff dog
This huge dog was first used to protect herds from wolves, leopards and bears in Tibet. 23

Toggenburg goat
The Toggenburg goat comes from Switzerland and is a dairy breed (used for its milk). 16

Toulouse goose
This famous French goose is grey with fluffy feathers that are often used in pillows and bedding. 20

Verata goat
From western Spain, the Verata goat is small with strong, long legs that enable it to live in mountains. 17

Vietnamese Pot-bellied pig
From Vietnam in Asia, this small pig has short legs and a belly that hangs down low. It has an upturned snout and small ears and eyes. 12

White Holland turkey
A very old breed of turkey, the White Holland has snow-white feathers and a red or bluish head. 21

White Pekin duck
The White Pekin is a type of duck bred in China and used mainly for meat. 20

Wyandotte chicken
This chicken was named for the Native American Wynadotte people. It lays brown eggs and its meat is yellow. 19

For Lucy & George

8
eightbooks

**Published in 2019 by
Eight Books Limited
40 Herbert Gardens
London NW10 3BU
info@8books.co.uk
www.8books.co.uk**

© Eight Books Limited 2019
Text © Mark Fletcher 2019
Illustrations © Jim Medway 2019

All rights reserved. No part of this publication may be reproduced or transmitted in any form or by any means, electronic, or mechanical, including photocopying, recording or by any information storage or retrieval system, without prior permission in writing from the publisher.

A catalogue record for this book is available from the British Library.
ISBN 978 1 9998583 4 6
Printed in China